HIDING FROM THE NAZIS

by David A. Adler

illustrated by Karen Ritz

Holiday House/New York

The author thanks Lore Baer for her cooperation in the preparation of this manuscript and Ann Shore of the Hidden Child Foundation/ADL at 823 United Nations Plaza, New York, NY 10017-3560.

Text copyright © 1997 by David A. Adler
Illustrations copyright © 1997 by Karen Ritz
ALL RIGHTS RESERVED
Printed in the United States of America
FIRST EDITION

Library of Congress Cataloging-in-Publication Data
Adler, David A.
Hiding from the Nazis / by David A. Adler; illustrated by Karen
Ritz. — 1st ed.
p.   cm.
Summary: The true story of Lore Baer who as a four-year-old Jewish
child was placed with a Christian family in the Dutch farm country
to avoid persecution by the Nazis.
ISBN 0-8234-1288-1
1. Baer, Lore, 1938–   —Juvenile literature. 2. Jewish children
in the Holocaust—Netherlands—Biography—Juvenile literature.
3. World War, 1939–1945—Jews—Rescue—Netherlands—Juvenile
literature.   4. Jews—Netherlands—Biography—Juvenile literature.
[1. Baer, Lore, 1938–   . 2. Jews—Netherlands—Biography.
3. World War, 1939–1945—Jews—Rescue. 4. Holocaust, Jewish
(1939–1945)—Netherlands.] I. Ritz, Karen, ill. II. Title.
DS135.N6B343   1997   96-38451   CIP   AC
940.53′18—dc20

Ernst Baer was born in Germany in 1907. His parents and grandparents had been born there, too. The Baers were loyal Germans. But in 1933, because he was Jewish, Ernst Baer felt he had to leave his homeland.

That January, Adolf Hitler, who was head of the Nazi party, had become chancellor, leader of the German government. Soon after he became chancellor, Jewish-owned stores were boycotted. Books written by Jews were burned. Jews were fired from their jobs. *Jews Not Wanted* signs were posted everywhere.

Ernst Baer no longer felt safe. He left his home, job, and the woman he loved, Edith Schmidt, and moved to Amsterdam, Holland. There he and his friend Herbert Gottschall opened a butcher shop.

In 1934 Edith Schmidt joined Ernst in Amsterdam. They married and with Herbert and his wife Erna, they rented a small house near the butcher shop.

The Baers were glad they had moved to Amsterdam.

During the next few years, more anti-Jewish laws were passed in Germany. Jews were no longer citizens. They were not even allowed to fly a German flag. Thousands of German Jews moved to Holland.

But the hatred the Baers escaped in Germany was spreading.

In the years since the Baers and the Gottschalls came to Amsterdam, Adolf Hitler was preparing for war. In March 1938 he sent German troops into neighboring Austria and declared it part of greater Germany. In the fall of 1938 Germany took over the Sudetenland, a section of Czechoslovakia. On September 1, 1939, German troops invaded Poland. Two days later, Britain and France declared war on Germany.

In 1938, the year of Germany's take-over of Austria and the Sudeten-land, the Gottschalls and Baers each had a baby.

Herbert Gottschall never saw his only child. Early in 1938 he suddenly died of a heart attack. His son Hans was born a few weeks later, in March. Edith and Ernst Baer's daughter Lore was born in August.

Soon after Lore Baer was born, her grandfather, Julius Schmidt, came to visit. Edith Baer was glad to have her father out of Germany. She convinced him to stay in Amsterdam, where she was sure he would be safe.

Julius Schmidt moved into the same house with the Baers and Gottschalls. During the day, while Ernst and Edith were at the butcher shop, he
took care of Lore. He pushed her carriage, and when Lore was older they
held hands and took long walks together.

Lore loved her grandfather. She called him Opa.

Lore loved to play, too. She and Hans shared toys, played house and doctor, and Lore's favorite game, hide-and-seek. Her best hiding place was under a blanket.

On May 10, 1940, German forces invaded Holland. A few days later the armies of Holland surrendered. Queen Wilhelmina and members of her government escaped to Britain.

Ernst Baer wanted to leave, too. He tried to get visas for himself and the others. But representatives of the United States and Cuba refused him.

Nazis followed the German army into Holland.

First came anti-Jewish laws. Jews could only shop between 3:00 PM and 5:00 PM. Their property was taken away. They lost their jobs. And beginning in May 1942, they were forced to wear a yellow star so everyone would know who was a Jew.

Then there were arrests.

The arrested Jews were sent to Westerbork, a transit and work camp in northeastern Holland. From there most were taken to death camps, to Auschwitz and Sobibor, where they were killed. At first the Nazis took only out-of-work Jews. Then they took everyone.

In March 1943 there was a loud knock on the Baers' door. Two uniformed Nazis with guns pushed their way into the house.

Lore ran behind the staircase and hid.

The Nazis showed Edith Baer some papers. They had come for Opa.

Edith Baer cried. She pleaded with the Nazis to spare her father. "You can't take him!" she screamed. "You can't!"

But they did.

Edith, Ernst, and Lore Baer never saw Opa again.

Opa was held at Westerbork for a few months. From there he was taken to Germany, to Bergen-Belsen, a concentration camp for Jewish prisoners, where he died.

Edith and Ernst Baer and Erna Gottschall knew the Nazis would be back. They decided to hide. They felt it would be safest if the children and their parents didn't hide together.

The Baers told Lore they were taking her to the apartment of Else and Sam Izaaks, a couple they knew from the butcher shop. But they didn't tell her why. They didn't want to frighten her. They just said, "Don't tell anyone your name is Baer and don't tell anyone you're Jewish."

Sam Izaaks was Jewish. His wife was Christian. But they had papers saying they both were Christians. The Izaakses promised to take care of Lore.

"Be good," Edith and Ernst told Lore. "We will see you soon." Then they were gone.

Lore was frightened. She was just four and a half years old. She didn't know why her parents had given her away. She thought she had done something wrong.

Lore was with the Izaakses for just one week. Then the Izaakses started to worry that their neighbors might find out they were hiding a Jewish child, or that Sam was Jewish. During the next few weeks they moved Lore several times. But Nazis were everywhere. Every day there were more arrests. No hiding place in Amsterdam seemed safe.

In April 1943 Sam Izaaks took Lore by train to Hoorn, the center of Dutch farm country. Two men on bicycles met them at the station. They told Lore her name would now be Lore Kruk. Then one of them put Lore on the handlebars of his bicycle and rode her to a new hiding place, the Schouten farm in nearby Oosterblokker.

People there didn't ask many questions about Lore. When they did, Ma and Pa Schouten said she was their niece and that her parents had to move to find work. When the little girl's parents were settled, they would come back for her.

The Schoutens had five grown children, three sons and two daughters. Their youngest daughter, Cornellia, was in her early twenties. She shared her room with Lore.

Cornellia was like a mother to her.

At night Lore was often frightened. She was sure that when she closed her eyes, Cornellia would leave, too. Cornellia held Lore so she could sleep.

The Schouten farm was a new world to Lore. She had been a city girl. Before she came to Oosterblokker she had never seen cows, sheep, or so much grass. She loved to run across the open fields. Cornellia taught Lore how to milk cows, bake bread, churn butter, and make cream.

On Sundays Lore went with the Schoutens to church, and beginning in 1944, she went to the church school. The children at the school didn't know Lore was Jewish, but the pastor did. He made sure Lore was safe.

Lore wasn't the only one hiding at the Schoutens. People running from
the Nazis often stopped there and stayed for a while.

Nazis came, too.

If there was a warning that Nazis were coming, Cornellia quickly took
Lore by bicycle to the next town, to Cornellia's sister's house. There they
waited until it was safe to go back.

Sometimes there was no time to get away.

Then Lore was taken into a closet. Under the floor boards was a secret tunnel. It led to a large box in the barn, inside the hayloft.

Hiding was no longer a game for Lore. She was frightened. Lore couldn't cough or sneeze. She had to remain very quiet so the Nazis wouldn't hear her.

Lore never hid alone. There were always other people with her inside the hayloft. But she couldn't see them. Sometimes she wondered if her parents were there, hiding with her in the dark.

Lore's second winter in hiding, the winter of 1944–1945, was a difficult one. Many people in Holland were without food. They came to the Dutch farmland with money, silver, jewelry, and other valuables hoping to trade for something to eat.

The Schoutens wouldn't take unfair payment from their countrymen. They gave their food generously.

But when Nazis and German soldiers came for food, the Schoutens said they had nothing, that the milk had gone sour, that their crops had spoiled.

By mid-1944 Germany was losing the war. On April 25, 1945, Russian forces surrounded Berlin, Germany's capital. On April 30, 1945, Adolf Hitler killed himself. Eight days later, May 8, 1945, was V-E Day, Victory-in-Europe Day. The armies of many nations had united to defeat the German army.

The Schoutens celebrated the end of the war. A few days later Cornellia told Lore that her parents were coming to take her home.

Lore was confused. She felt the farm *was* her home. She wanted to stay with Cornellia and the Schoutens. She wanted to stay in Oosterblokker.

Edith and Ernst Baer had dreamed for two years about the day they would see their child again. They thought Lore would run into their arms.

She didn't.

When the Baers came for Lore, she hid again, this time from her parents. Lore hid behind her beloved Cornellia.

Edith and Ernst Baer stayed with the Schoutens for a few days, so Lore would become comfortable with them. They explained to Lore that she had done nothing wrong. They had brought her to the Izaakses so she would be safe, because they loved her.

Edith and Ernst had been hiding near Oosterblokker. After V-E Day they contacted Else and Sam Izaaks who told them where to find Lore.

Lore's friend Hans Gottschall and his mother Erna also survived. Hans had hidden with a Christian family in The Hague, the capital city of Holland. Erna hid, too, in the Amsterdam apartment of a Christian woman she knew from the butcher shop. A uniformed Nazi, a member of the feared SS squad, lived in the building. Erna Gottschall could not move freely in the apartment. She had to keep away from windows. She never went outside.

After a few days at the Schoutens, Edith, Ernst, and Lore Baer returned to Amsterdam. They were done hiding. They were together again.

In 1947 the Baers moved to the United States.

Even here, Edith Baer was afraid of losing her child again. Each morning before school, Edith made Lore promise to wave to her at lunch time. Edith worked in a nearby factory and every day at noon, she stopped work, and looked out the window for Lore.

It took Lore many years to learn to trust and love her parents again. But at least she was safe. She had survived the Holocaust.

Author's Note

Before the German invasion in May 1940, there were 140,000 Jews living in Holland. Of this number, 23,000 were refugees from Germany. One of the first Nazi decrees in Holland was that all Jews who had entered the country after January 1933 be sent to concentration camps and their property confiscated. This led to the arrest of Julius Schmidt, Lore's beloved Opa.

Of the Jews living in Holland, between 106,000 to 107,000 were sent to Nazi death camps, where more than 100,000 of them were murdered. Some Jews were able to leave the country. An estimated 22,000 to 25,000 Jews hid and almost half of them survived the war.

The Gottschalls moved to the United States in 1947, the same year the Baers came here. The Baer and Gottschall families have remained close friends.

In 1950 the Baers had a second child, Lillian.

Lore Baer works now as an artist and art therapist. She is a wife, mother, and grandmother. She has gone back to Oosterblokker a few times to visit and to thank the Schoutens for opening their hearts and their home to her—for saving her life.

At a 1992 session, the Commission for the Designation of the Righteous chose to honor Theodorus (Pa), Maria (Ma), and Cornellia Shouten with the Medal of the Righteous Among the Nations. Their names were engraved on the honor wall in the Garden of the Righteous at Yad Vashem in Jerusalem, Israel. In March 1995, for their noble deeds, they were made honorary citizens of Israel.